1363
This edition published in 1993 by Tiger Books International PLC, London
© 1987 Coombe Books
Printed and bound in Hong Kong
All rights reserved
ISBN 1-85501-125-5

ENGLAND
FROM THE AIR

TIGER BOOKS INTERNATIONAL
LONDON

First port of call for today's visitor from Europe, Canterbury (previous pages) was journey's end for generations of pilgrims, and now marks the beginning or end of days-long hikes for downland walkers. The soaring spires of its impressive cathedral mark and distinguish the city to the traveller on the ground, and even from the air dominate the huddle of thousands of lesser buildings which appear to be kept at bay only by the definitive, encircling road system. Charles Dickens passed through on his way to Broadstairs (these pages) to take up residence in the castellated Victorian house on the cliff edge (top right). Here he wrote *David Copperfield*, while the building itself, despite its proximity to the bright, sandy sweep of the bay, inspired another novel, *Bleak House*.

From Kent, the route into London may take you over Tower Bridge (overleaf). Confident and ornate, it leads to the cradle of London's post-Conquest history – the Tower itself. Flanking this superb, beautifully preserved legacy of the past are reminders of the present: the edges of the bustling density of the City's commercial centre (left), and the beginnings of the residential sprawl of the East End's former docklands.

Those elderly gentlemen in scarlet coats and black tricorn hats, pottering contentedly around London, reside in arguably the most famous 66 acres in London – Chelsea's Royal Hospital (previous pages). Brick-built to Sir Christopher Wren's design by 1692, its quiet grandeur is enlivened by stone window-dressings, cornerstones and portico. Along the site's north front runs the road that bears its name – Royal Hospital Road – and which separates it from the gardens and residential area of South Kensington (top left). Immediately west of the Hospital is the National Army Museum.

Hampton Court Palace (these pages) was enlarged in the late 17th century, and the mark of Wren is again immediately evident in the tall, square extension to the old Tudor structure. A rabbit-warren of a palace, the original bristles with brick chimneys, turrets and castellations – an apt memorial to the ostentatious Cardinal Wolsey who built it. Formal Restoration landscaping emphasises the dual personality of the Thames-side site. Landscaping of a different sort brings hundreds of thousands to London's Kew Gardens each year, where educational and recreational benefits abound. Dotted by their magnificent hothouses (overleaf), the three hundred acres provide a welcome breathing space amid the expanding London conurbation.

One of the most celebrated of many sporting sites on London's fringes, Wimbledon (previous pages) is the headquarters of the All England Lawn Tennis and Croquet Club. For two weeks each year, its two dozen grass and hard courts echo to the sound of ball upon racquet, the stentorian call of umpires, and the applause of thousands of devotees of world tennis. Centre Court, and Court No 1, each with comprehensive spectator facilities, dwarf the others, but the sunny luxuriance of green overall never fails to recall that inimitable fortnight of delights, from strawberries to silver trophies.

Twenty miles further south-west lies Guildford (these pages), with its steeply rising High Street virtually bisecting this photograph laterally. Among the most classic Georgian main streets in the south of England, its pride and joy is the huge clock suspended over it from the side of the 17th-century Town Hall. Of Guildford's more modern landmarks, the post-War cathedral sits grandly aloof on elevated ground to the west.

Meanwhile, Bodiam Castle (overleaf) stands proudly in is moat, almost anachronistic among the careful lines of the modern rural Sussex landscape. A tribute to the earliest attempts to combine residential comforts with military defence, it seems the perfect, most regularly proportioned of English medieval castles.

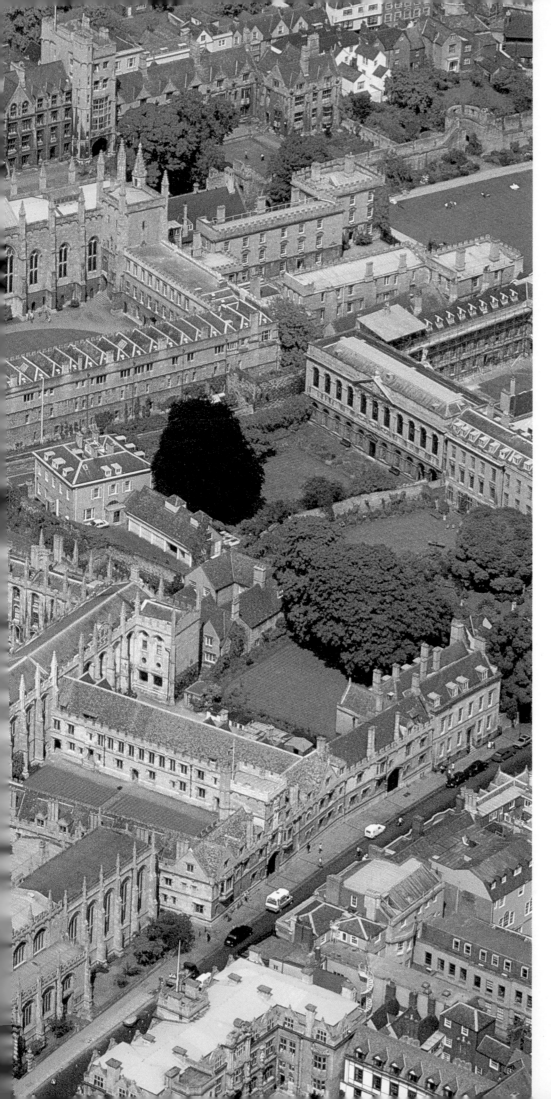

Some thirty miles to the north-west of London lies the quiet village-town of Marlow (previous pages). The epitome of fashionable Buckinghamshire, its spacious riverside gardens and leisurely through-traffic of Thames sailing-craft endow it with a placid, timeless and still very rural charm.

A further thirty miles north-west is England's educational capital – Oxford (these pages) – with its 'dreaming spires and pinnacles'. The bold, 14th-century spire of St Mary the Virgin (centre foreground) faces the squat Oriel College on the opposite side of the 'High', and vies with the burgeoning dome of the Radcliffe Camera (now a library). Between them rises All Souls College with its immaculately tended quadrangle. William of Wykeham's slightly larger New College – one of the first built in Oxford – lies by Hertford College, where students are enjoying the midday sun in the oak-dominated courtyard. Queen's College stands to the right of New.

One dreaming spire is enough for Salisbury (overleaf), in neighbouring Wiltshire: its cathedral boasts the tallest in England – at 404 feet – as well as the most complete, unadulterated medieval design. Its square, tree-lined close gives residents of the adjacent North and West Walks admirable vistas, and marks a break between the main city (right) and the suburbs of Harnham, along with the wide expanse of pasture where the Nadder (top left) joins the Avon.

The 12th-century town plan of the original Stratford-upon-Avon (previous pages) – three streets parallel with, and three at right-angles to, the river – remains unchanged despite successive rebuilding and continuing development. Meanwhile, the 18th-century spire of Holy Trinity, the riverside church where Shakespeare was baptised and is buried, proclaims the modern community's link with the bard. Further up-river stands the Royal Shakespeare Theatre – a solid, 1930s structure, complete with picture gallery and museum, which replaced a Victorian predecessor destroyed by fire.

Centrepieces in vastly-industrialised Coventry (these pages) are the old and new cathedrals: the flat-roofed building designed by Basil Spence and completed in 1962 (centre) has a clear-glass west screen affording worshippers sight of the bombed shell of the old, with only its Gothic spire and pentagonal sanctuary remaining.

Between Stratford and Coventry lies the fine old town of Warwick (overleaf), guarded on the Avon by its medieval castle in one of Capability Brown's sweeping landscaped settings. In the centre of the town the Norman church of St Mary, mostly rebuilt around 1700, sports a pseudo-Gothic tower – an attempt by its restorers to retain the medieval flavour of the original.

In the 1950s redevelopment of Birmingham's city centre began (previous pages) – a difficult undertaking if disruption of the lives of over a million people was to be avoided. Most of that work is now complete and, for all its inevitable density, the city offers an enviable combination of commercial and industrial opportunity. Access is a priority, with swingeing ring-road systems and two main stations – New Street (far left) and Moor Street (centre foreground) – in the heart of the scheme, close to the famous Bull Ring Centre (bottom left).

But to get away from it all you could do worse than travel north to Rydal Water (these pages) in the southern Lake District. A paradise for fell-walkers and short-distance ramblers alike, the area is alive with the sights, sounds and smells of nature virtually untouched by man. Elevated woodlands (right) support fir, oak, birch, beech and sycamore, and offer superb views of the lake with its main feature, Heron Island. Beyond lies its neighbouring lake, Grasmere, and the village of that name is just visible to the right. The wilder attractions of Helvellyn (overleaf) await the northbound traveller; its broad, masculine surface (left) is highlighted by fine winter snow, while the waters of Thirlmere reflect the raw climate of the heart of Lakeland.

The magnificent hilltop cathedral at Lincoln (previous pages) is visible for up to forty miles of the surrounding, flat, rich fenland. Its Norman origins match the Conqueror's castle beyond, while its ornate Gothic architecture is as impressive within as without. The Bishop's Palace, to its left, watches over the old Roman town, while the lower ground is dominated by Victorian development (left), and the uphill plateau by more modern building (right). Beyond lies the Carholme, where for years the Lincoln Handicap was run to begin the flat-racing season.

Well south of Lincoln, Oxford's rival university, Cambridge (these pages), is compact yet uncrowded. The River Cam winds between successive colleges – St John's (top left); then Trinity; King's, with its towering, pinnacled chapel (centre); and Queen's. With its liberal complement of churches, chapels, museums, fine terraces and busy, well-facilitated shopping centre, Cambridge possesses universal appeal.

Across to the east stands one of England's most exquisite stately homes – Holkham Hall (overleaf), owned by the Earls of Leicester for 250 years, and built to harmonise with the graceful, barely undulating Norfolk landscape. Reminiscent of some Italian palace, its Palladian design and formal gardens recall an age of luxury and elegance. Once again, the aerial view perfectly demonstrates the blend of the works of man and nature which gives England such enviable and satisfying landscapes.